Selected from

WINDMILLS
— of —
THE GODS

Sidney Sheldon

Supplementary Material by
Edward Lavitt
and the staff of Literacy
Volunteers of New York City

WRITERS' VOICES
Literacy Volunteers of
New York City

WRITERS' VOICES ® was made possible by grants from: An anonymous foundation; The Vincent Astor Foundation; Booth Ferris Foundation; Exxon Corporation; James Money Management, Inc.; Knight Foundation; Philip Morris Companies Inc.; Scripps Howard Foundation; The House of Seagram and H.W. Wilson Foundation.

ATTENTION READERS: We would like to hear what you think about our books. Please send your comments or suggestions to:

The Editors
Literacy Volunteers of New York City
121 Avenue of the Americas
New York, NY 10013

Selection: From WINDMILLS OF THE GODS by Sidney Sheldon. Copyright © 1987 by Sheldon Literary Trust. By permission of William Morrow & Company, Inc.

Supplementary materials © 1991 by Literacy Volunteers of New York City Inc.

Printed in the United States of America.

97 96 95 94 93 92 91   10 9 8 7 6 5 4 3 2 1

First LVNYC Printing: March 1991

ISBN 0-929631-32-3

Writers' Voices is a series of books published by Literacy Volunteers of New York City Inc., 121 Avenue of the Americas, New York, NY 10013. The words, "Writers' Voices," are a trademark of Literacy Volunteers of New York City.

Cover designed by Paul Davis Studio; interior designed by Caron Harris.

Executive Director, LVNYC: Eli Zal
Publishing Director, LVNYC: Nancy McCord
Managing Editor: Sarah Kirshner
Publishing Coordinator: Yvette Martinez-Gonzalez

LVNYC is an affiliate of Literacy Volunteers of America.

Acknowledgments

Literacy Volunteers of New York City gratefully acknowledges the generous support of the following foundations and corporations that made the publication of WRITERS' VOICES and NEW WRITERS' VOICES possible: An anonymous foundation; The Vincent Astor Foundation; Booth Ferris Foundation; Exxon Corporation; James Money Management, Inc.; Knight Foundation; Philip Morris Companies Inc.; Scripps Howard Foundation; The House of Seagram and H.W. Wilson Foundation.

This book could not have been realized without the kind and generous cooperation of the author, Sidney Sheldon, and his publisher, William Morrow & Company, Inc. Thanks also to Lisa Queen, editor.

We deeply appreciate the contributions of the following suppliers: Cam Steel Die Rule Works Inc. (steel cutting die for display); Boise Cascade Canada Ltd. (text stock); Black Dot Graphics (text typesetting); Horizon Paper Company and Manchester Paper Company (cover stock); MCUSA (display header); Delta Corrugated Container (corrugated display); J.A.C. Lithographers (cover color separations); and Offset Paperback Mfrs., Inc., A Bertelsmann Company (cover and text printing and binding).

For their guidance, support and hard work, we are indebted to the LVNYC Board of Directors' Publishing Committee: James E. Galton, Marvel Entertainment Group; Virginia Barber, Virginia Barber Literary

Agency, Inc.; Doris Bass, Bantam Doubleday Dell; Jeff Brown; Jerry Butler, William Morrow & Company, Inc.; George P. Davidson, Ballantine Books; Joy M. Gannon, St. Martin's Press; Walter Kiechel, *Fortune*; Geraldine E. Rhoads, Diamandis Communications Inc.; Virginia Rice, Reader's Digest; Martin Singerman, News America Publishing, Inc.; James L. Stanko, James Money Management, Inc. and F. Robert Stein, Pryor, Cashman, Sherman & Flynn.

Thanks also to Joy M. Gannon and Julia Weil of St. Martin's Press for producing this book; Jerry Butler for assistance in obtaining permission; Venas Matthews-Carroll for carefully choosing the selection; Edward Lavitt for his skill and diligence in the research and writing of the supplementary material for this book; Andrea Connolly for her thoughtful copyediting and suggestions; and Helen Morris for her dedication and her helpful contributions at so many stages of the book. Thanks also to Ambassador Herbert S. Okun, Department of State, and Gary Ink of *Publishers Weekly* for help with research.

Our thanks to Paul Davis Studio and Myrna Davis, Paul Davis, Jeanine Esposito, Alex Ginns and Frank Begrowicz for their inspired design of the covers of these books. Thanks also to Caron Harris for her sensitive design of the interior of this book, Karen Bernath for design of maps and diagrams, and Ron Bel Bruno for his timely help.

And finally, special credit must be given to Marilyn Boutwell, Jean Fargo and Gary Murphy of the LVNYC staff for their contributions to the educational and editorial content of these books.

Contents

Note to the Reader

Windmills of the Gods is a best-selling novel by Sidney Sheldon. It is a good example of the kind of exciting, fast-paced story that many readers enjoy. These stories have lots of action and often are set in exotic places. They are sometimes called "thrillers."

Every writer has a special voice. That is why we call our series *Writers' Voices*. We chose *Windmills of the Gods* because Sidney Sheldon's voice can be clearly heard as he creates a story filled with realistic detail and suspense. In making selections from the book, we chose to follow the character of Mary Ashley, a professor and a mother who suddenly becomes an important part of world events.

Reading "About the Selections from

Windmills of the Gods" on page 11 will help you to begin thinking about what you will read in the selections.

In addition to selections from *Windmills of the Gods*, this book includes chapters with interesting and helpful information related to the story. You may read these before or after reading the story. You may choose to read some or all of these chapters.

- If you would like more information about Romania, the country in which the story is set, look at the chapter called "About Romania" on page 54.
- If you would like more information about why and how books become bestsellers, look at the chapter called "About Bestsellers" on page 59.
- Many readers enjoy finding out about the person who wrote the story. Sometimes this information will give you more insight into the story. You can find out more about Sidney Sheldon in the chapter on page 50.

If you are a new reader, you may want to have this book read aloud to you, perhaps more than once. Even if you are a more experienced reader, you may enjoy hearing it read aloud before reading it silently to yourself.

We encourage you to read *actively*. Here are some things you can do.

Before Reading

- Read the front and back covers of the book, and look at the cover illustration. Ask yourself what you expect the book to be about.
- Think about why you want to read this book. Perhaps you have seen a TV mini-series based on one of Sidney Sheldon's books.
- Look at the Contents page. See where you can find a map of Romania and other information. Decide what you want to read and in what order.

During Reading

- There may be difficult words and Romanian names and places that are unfamiliar to you. Keep reading to see if the meaning becomes clear. If it doesn't, go back and reread the difficult part or discuss it with others. Or look up the words in the dictionary.
- Ask yourself questions as you read. For example: What would it be like to suddenly find yourself in a foreign country?

After Reading

- Think about what you have read. Did you identify with the main character, Mary Ashley? Did the events of the story change your thinking about world affairs?
- Talk with others about your thoughts.
- Try some of the questions and activities in "Questions for the Reader" on page 46. They are meant to help you discover more about what you have read and how it relates to you.

The editors of *Writers' Voices* hope you will write to us. We want to know your thoughts about our books.

About
the Selections
from
Windmills
of the Gods

In Sidney Sheldon's novel *Windmills of the Gods*, Mary Ashley is appointed American ambassador to Romania, an Eastern European country. She had been a college professor in Kansas. The new president of the United States, Paul Ellison, chooses Mary to be ambassador because he has read her writings on the Communist countries of Eastern Europe. Mary has never been to Romania but she feels an emotional tie with the country because her grandfather was born there.

After her confirmation by the United States Senate, Mary, a widow, and her two young children arrive in Bucharest, the capital of Romania. When a new ambassador arrives in a foreign capital, he or she must make an appointment with the head of the foreign state and formally present his or her credentials. The head of state—president, king, chief—then officially accepts the new ambassador.

Although *Windmills of the Gods* is fiction, it is based on many historical and political facts. It is important to keep in mind that Sidney Sheldon has been inspired by real events and real people but that the story he weaves comes from his imagination. The events did not really happen, but perhaps they could have. In this discussion of the selections, we will touch on some of the things that are fact and some that are fiction.

Every major capital city in the world has ambassadors from other countries living there. These ambassadors and their staffs (also known as diplomats) represent their governments on a day-to-day basis in matters of mutual concern to both countries, such as trade and issues of war and peace. There are about 150 foreign embassies in Washington, D.C.

An embassy is the official building for the ambassador and diplomatic staff. Since even the most well-prepared ambassador cannot know everything about a host country, he or she has expert staff to study and analyze important matters. These specialists keep track of agriculture, commerce, industry and, of course, military and political matters.

Each United States embassy has a special communications section for sending messages to and receiving messages from Washington, D.C. Many of these messages contain secret information about the host country that is gathered by the Central Intelligence Agency (CIA). Each United States embassy has one or more CIA agents whose job is to collect as much information as possible about the foreign country. The information is sent to the United States president so that he and his staff can be prepared to make decisions based on as many facts as possible. Often the ambassador may not even know which staff members are also agents for the CIA.

In the selections, Ambassador Mary Ashley feels that some of the embassy staff resent her. The main reason for this is that Mary is a political appointee and that the embassy staff is made up of career diplomats. These professionals sometimes resent an ambassador who has not worked his or her way up through the ranks. At one point in the book, Harriet Kruger, a member of Mary's diplomatic staff, explains to Mary that, for the staff, "You're an amateur telling professionals how to run their business."

However, Mary is an expert on Eastern Europe and is well suited for the responsibilities of the ambassadorship. She is familiar with the culture, language, government and history of Romania.

This selection from *Windmills of the Gods* is set in the recent past, sometime before 1989. At that time, many countries in Eastern Europe, including Romania, had Communist governments allied with the Soviet Union. These countries were said to be "behind the iron curtain." This saying referred to the strict control of these countries by the Soviet Union. The United States through its ambassadors tried to keep the lines of communication to these countries open by arranging for trade with them.

Some Communist countries had harsh rulers. Romania at this time was ruled by President Nicolae Ceausescu, a powerful and feared leader. The fictional Romanian president in *Windmills of the Gods*, Alexandru Ionescu, has many things in common with Ceausescu.

The KGB, the Soviet Union's secret police, had agents in each of these countries. (The initials stand for the Russian words for *Committee of State Security*.) Each country also had its own secret police who worked with the KGB. In Romania the secret police were called the Securitate. Embassies in foreign countries must hire local citizens to do housekeeping and other jobs. It was common knowledge that, in the Communist countries, many of the drivers, gardeners, cleaners and other employees of the embassy were members of the Securitate or the KGB.

Today the countries of Eastern Europe have broken many of their ties to the Soviet Union. Many of them are moving toward having democratic governments. In Romania, Ceausescu was executed in 1989.

As the story opens, Mary has just arrived in Romania.

President Ellison and his foreign advisor, Stanton Rogers, had wished her well when she left Washington. Stanton Rogers will be Mary's Washington contact with the president.

The only person Mary knows in Romania is Mike Slade. She met him in Washington but now he is attached to the embassy.

Perhaps reading the selections will remind you of a time when you faced a challenging new job. Or perhaps it might make you think about what it is like to live in a country without democracy.

MAPS OF PLACES MENTIONED IN THE SELECTIONS

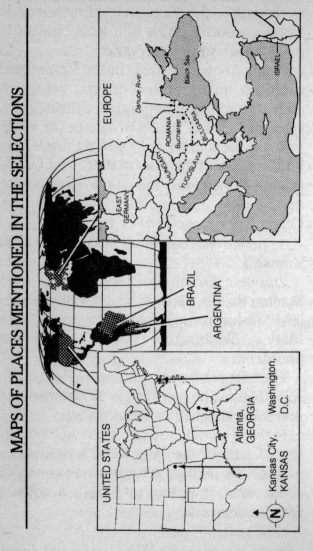

Selected from

Windmills
of
the Gods

Sidney Sheldon

The drive from the airport to the city was fascinating. They drove on a two-lane highway heavily traveled by trucks and automobiles, but every few miles the traffic would be held up by little gypsy carts plodding along the road. On both sides of the highway were modern factories next to ancient huts. The car passed farm after farm, with women working in the fields, colorful bandannas knotted around their heads.

They drove by Băneasa, Bucharest's domestic airport. Just beyond it, off the main highway, was a low, blue and gray, two-story building with an ominous look about it.

"What is that?" Mary asked.

Florian grimaced. "The Ivan Stelian

Prison. That is where they put anyone who disagrees with the Romanian government."

During the drive, Colonel McKinney pointed to a red button near the door. "This is an emergency switch," he explained. "If you're ever in trouble—attacked by terrorists or whomever—just press this button. It activates a radio transmitter in the car that's monitored at the embassy, and turns on a red light on the roof of the car. We're able to triangulate your position within minutes."

Mary said fervently, "I hope I'll never have to use it."

"I hope so too, Madam Ambassador."

The center of Bucharest was beautiful. There were parks and monuments and fountains everywhere one looked. She was in the homeland of her forefathers.

The streets were crowded with people and buses and streetcars. The limousine honked its way through the traffic, the pedestrians scurrying out of the way, as the car turned into a small, tree-lined street.

The American embassy in Bucharest, at 21 Şoseaua Kiseleff, is a white semi-Gothic two-story building with an iron gate in front, patrolled by a uniformed officer with a gray coat and a red hat. A second guard sits inside a security booth at the side of the gate.

Inside, the lobby is ornate. It has a marble floor, two closed-circuit television sets at a desk guarded by a marine, and a fireplace with a fire screen on which is painted a dragon breathing smoke. The corridors are lined with portraits of presidents. A winding staircase leads to the second floor, where a conference room and offices are located.

A marine guard was waiting for Mary.

She followed him upstairs to a reception room where a middle-aged woman sat behind a desk.

She rose. "Good morning, Madam Ambassador. I'm Dorothy Stone, your secretary."

"How do you do?"

Dorothy said, "I'm afraid you have quite a crowd in there."

She opened the office door, and Mary walked into the room. There were nine people seated around a large conference table. They rose as Mary entered. They were all staring at her, and Mary felt a wave of animosity that was almost palpable. The first person she saw was Mike Slade. She thought of the dream she had had.

"I see you got here safely," Mike said. "Let me introduce you to your department heads."

"Please be seated," Mary said. She moved to the seat at the head of the table and surveyed the group. *Hostility comes in all ages, sizes, and shapes,* Mary thought.

Mike Slade was saying, "All of us are serving at your discretion. You can replace any of us at any time."

That's a lie, Mary thought angrily. *I tried to replace you.*

The meeting lasted fifteen minutes. There was general inconsequential conversation.

Mike Slade finally said, "Dorothy will set up individual meetings for all of you with the ambassador later in the day. Thank you."

Mary resented his taking charge. When she and Slade were alone, Mary asked, "Which one of them is the CIA agent attached to the embassy?"

Mike looked at her a moment and said, "Why don't you come with me?"

He walked out of the office. Mary hesitated a moment, and then went after him. She followed him down a long corridor, past a rabbit warren of offices. He came to a large door with a marine guard standing in front of it. The guard stepped aside as Mike pushed the door open. He turned and gestured for Mary to enter.

She stepped inside and looked around. The room was an incredible combination of metal and glass, covering the floor, the walls, and the ceiling.

Mike Slade closed the heavy door behind them. "This is the Bubble Room. Every embassy in an iron curtain country has one. It's the only room in the embassy that can't be bugged."

He saw her look of disbelief.

"Madam Ambassador, not only is the embassy bugged, but you can bet your last dollar that your residence is bugged, and that if you go out to a restaurant for dinner, your table will be bugged. You're in enemy territory."

Mary sank into a chair. "How do you handle that?" she asked. "I mean not ever being able to talk freely?"

"We do an electronic sweep every morning. We find their bugs and pull them out. Then they replace them, and we pull *those* out."

"Why do we permit Romanians to work in the embassy?"

"It's their playground. They're the home team. We play by their rules, or blow the ball game. They can't get their microphones into this room because there are marine guards on duty in front of that door twenty-four hours a day. Now—what are your questions?"

"I just wondered who the CIA man was."

"Eddie Maltz, your political counselor."

"Is he the only CIA man on the staff?"

"Yes."

Was there a hesitation in his voice?

Mike Slade looked at his watch. "You're due to present your credentials in thirty minutes. Florian is waiting for you outside. Take your letter of credence. You'll give the original to President Ionescu and put a copy in our safe."

Mary found that she was gritting her teeth. "I *know* that, Mr. Slade."

"He requested that you bring the children with you. I've sent a car for them."

Without consulting her. "Thank you."

Headquarters for the Romanian government is a forbidding-looking building made of blocks of sandstone in the center of Bucharest. It is protected by a steel wall, with armed guards in front of it. There were more guards at the entrance to the building. An aide escorted Mary and the children upstairs.

President Alexandru Ionescu greeted Mary and the children in a long, rectangular-shaped room on the second floor. The President of Romania had a powerful presence. He was dark, with hawklike features and curly black hair. He had one of the most imperious noses she had ever seen. His eyes were blazing, mesmerizing.

The aide said, "Your Excellency, may I present Madam Ambassador from the United States?"

The President took Mary's hand and gave it a lingering kiss. "You are even more beautiful than your photographs."

"Thank you, Your Excellency. This is my daughter, Beth, and my son, Tim."

"Fine-looking children," Ionescu said. He looked at her expectantly. "You have something for me?"

Mary had almost forgotten. She quickly opened her purse and took out the letter of credence from President Ellison.

Alexandru Ionescu gave it a careless glance. "Thank you. I accept it on behalf of the Romanian government. You are now officially the American ambassador to my country." He beamed at her. "I have arranged a reception this evening for you. You will meet some of our people who will be working with you."

"That's very kind of you," Mary said.

He took her hand in his again and said, "We have a saying here. 'An ambassador arrives in tears because he knows he will be spending years in a foreign place, away from his friends, but when he leaves, he leaves in tears because he must leave his new friends in a country he has grown fond of.' I hope you will grow to love our country, Madam Ambassador." He massaged her hand.

"I'm sure I will." *He thinks I'm just another pretty face,* Mary thought grimly. *I'll have to do something about that.*

Mary sent the children home and spent the rest of the day at the embassy in the large conference room, meeting with the section heads, the political, economic, agriculture, administrative, and commerce counselors. Colonel McKinney was present as the military attaché.

They were all seated around a long, rectangular table.

It was the turn of Ted Thompson, the agriculture counselor. "The Romanian agriculture minister is in worse trouble than he's admitting. They're going to have a disastrous crop this year, and we can't afford to let them go under."

The economic counselor, Patricia Hatfield, protested, "We've given them enough aid, Ted. Romania's already operating under a favored-nations treaty. It's a GSP country." She looked at Mary, covertly.

She's doing this deliberately, Mary thought, *trying to embarrass me.*

Patricia Hatfield said, patronizingly, "A GSP country is—"

"—is a generalized system of preferences," Mary cut in. "We treat Romania as a less-developed country so that they get import and export advantages."

Hatfield's expression changed. "That's right," she said. "We're already giving the store away and—"

David Victor, the commerce counselor, interrupted. "We're not giving it away—we're just trying to keep it open so we can shop there. They need more credit in order to buy corn from us. If *we* don't sell it to them, they're going to buy it from Argentina." He turned to Mary. "It looks like we're going to lose out on soybeans. The Brazilians are trying to undercut us. I would appreciate it if you'd talk to the prime minister as soon as possible and try to make a package deal before we're shut out."

Mary looked over at Mike Slade, who was seated at the opposite end of the table slouched in his chair, doodling on a pad, seemingly paying no attention. "I'll see what I can do," Mary promised.

The cocktail party that afternoon was held at the Romanian State Palace for a visiting dignitary from East Germany.

As soon as Mary arrived, President Ionescu walked over to her. He kissed her hand and said, "I have been looking forward to seeing you again."

"Thank you, Your Excellency. I too."

She had a feeling he had been drinking heavily. She recalled the dossier on him: *Married. One son, fourteen, the heir apparent, and three daughters. Is a womanizer. Drinks a lot. A shrewd peasant mentality. Charming when it suits him. Generous to his friends. Dangerous and ruthless to his enemies.* Mary thought: *A man to beware of.*

Ionescu took Mary's arm and led her off to a deserted corner. "You will find us Romanians interesting." He squeezed her arm. "We are a very passionate people." He looked at her for a reaction, and when he got none, he went on. "For centuries, we have been Europe's doormat. The country with rubber borders. The Huns, Goths, Avars, Slavs, and Mongols wiped their feet on us, but Romania survived. And do you know how?" He leaned closer to her, and she could smell the liquor on his breath. "By giving our people a strong, firm leadership. They trust me, and I rule them well."

Mary thought of some of the stories she had heard. The arrests in the middle of the night, the kangaroo court, the atrocities, the disappearances.

As Ionescu went on talking, Mary looked over his shoulder at the people in the crowded room. There were at least two hundred, and Mary was sure they represented every embassy in Romania. She would meet them all soon.

A man came up to President Ionescu and whispered in his ear. The expression on Ionescu's face turned cold. He hissed something in Romanian, and the man nodded and hurried off. The dictator turned back to Mary, oozing charm again. "I must leave you now. I look forward to seeing you again soon."

And Ionescu was gone.

* * *

Mike took a sip of his coffee. "I understand that you had a nice chat with our fearless leader last night."

"President Ionescu? Yes. He seemed very pleasant."

"Oh, he is. He's a lovely fellow. Until he gets annoyed with somebody. Then he chops your head off."

Mary said nervously, "Shouldn't we talk about this in the Bubble Room?"

"Not necessary. I had your office swept for bugs this morning. It's clean. After the janitors and cleaning people come in, then watch out. By the way, don't let Ionescu's charm fool you. He's a dyed-in-the-wool son of a bitch. His people despise him, but there's nothing they can do about it. The secret police are everywhere. It's the KGB and police force wrapped into one. The general rule of thumb here is that one out of every three persons works for Securitate or the KGB. Romanians have orders not to have any contact with foreigners. If a foreigner wants to have dinner at a Romanian's apartment, it has to be approved first by the state."

Mary felt a shiver go through her.

"A Romanian can be arrested for signing a petition, criticizing the government, writing graffiti . . ."

Mary had read newspaper and magazine articles about repression in Communist countries, but living in the midst of it gave her a feeling of unreality.

"They do have trials here," Mary said.

"Oh, occasionally they'll have show trials, where reporters from the West are allowed to watch. But most of the people arrested manage to have fatal accidents while they're in police custody. There are gulags [prison camps] in Romania that we're not allowed to see. They're in the Delta area, and in the Danube near the Black Sea. I've talked to people who have seen them. The conditions there are horrifying."

"And there's no place they can escape to," Mary said, thinking aloud. "They have the Black Sea to the east, Bulgaria to the south, and Yugoslavia and Hungary on their other borders. They're right in the middle of the iron curtain."

"Ionescu is squeezing the people where it hurts. They're afraid to strike because they know they'll be shot. The standard of living here is one of the lowest in Europe. There's a shortage of everything. If the people see a line in front of a store, they'll join in and buy whatever it is that's for sale while they have the chance."

"It seems to me," Mary said slowly, "that all these things add up to a wonderful opportunity for us to help them."

Mike Slade looked at her. "Sure," he said, dryly. "Wonderful."

* * *

Every morning when Mary rode to work she noticed long lines of people outside the gates waiting to get into the consular section of the embassy. She had taken it for granted that they were people with minor problems they hoped the consul could solve. But on this particular morning she went to the window to take a closer look and the expressions she saw on their faces compelled her to go into Mike's office.

"Who are all those people waiting in line outside?"

Mike walked with her to the window. "They're mostly Romanian Jews. They're waiting to file applications for visas."

"But there's an Israeli embassy in Bucharest. Why don't they go there?"

"Two reasons," Mike explained. "First of all, they think the United States government has a greater chance of assisting them to get to Israel than the Israeli government. And secondly, they think there's less of a chance of the Romanian security people finding out their intention if they come to us. They're wrong, of course." He pointed out the window. "There's an apartment house directly across from the embassy that has several flats filled with agents using telescopic lenses, photographing everybody who goes in and out of the embassy."

"That's terrible!"

"That's the way they play the game. When a Jewish family applies for a visa to emigrate, they lose their green job cards and they're thrown out of their apartments. Their neighbors are instructed to turn their backs on them. Then it takes three to four years before the government will tell them whether they'll even get their exit papers, and the answer is usually no."

"Can't we do something about it?"

"We try all the time. But Ionescu enjoys playing a cat-and-mouse game with the Jews. Very few of them are ever allowed to leave the country."

Mary looked out at the expressions of hopelessness on their faces. "There has to be a way," Mary said.

"Don't break your heart," Mike told her.

* * *

David Victor, the commerce counselor, hurried into Mary's office. "I'm afraid I have some very bad news. I just got a tip that President Ionescu is going to approve a contract with Argentina for a million and a half tons of corn and with Brazil for half a million tons of soybeans. We were counting heavily on those deals."

"How far have the negotiations gone?"

"They're almost concluded. We've been shut out. I was about to send a cable to Washington—with your approval, of course," he added hastily.

"Hold off a bit," Mary said. "I want to think about it."

"You won't get President Ionescu to change

his mind. Believe me, I've tried every argument I could think of."

"Then we have nothing to lose if I give it a try." She buzzed her secretary. "Dorothy, set up an appointment with President Ionescu as quickly as possible."

Alexandru Ionescu invited Mary to the palace for lunch. As she entered she was greeted by Nicu, the President's fourteen-year-old son.

"Good afternoon, Madam Ambassador," he said. "I am Nicu. Welcome to the palace."

"Thank you."

He was a handsome boy, tall for his age, with beautiful black eyes and a flawless complexion. He had the bearing of an adult.

"I have heard very nice things about you," Nicu said.

"I'm pleased to hear that, Nicu."

"I will tell my father you have arrived."

Mary and Ionescu sat across from each other in the formal dining room, just the two of them. Mary wondered where his wife was. She seldom appeared, even at formal functions.

The President had been drinking and was in a mellow mood. He lighted a Snagov, the vile-smelling Romanian-made cigarette.

"I understand you have been doing some sight-seeing with your children."

"Yes, Your Excellency. Romania is such a beautiful country, and there is so much to see."

He gave her what he thought was a seductive smile. "One of these days you must let me show you my country." His smile became a parody of a leer. "I am an excellent guide. I could show you many interesting things."

"I'm sure you could," Mary said. "Mr. President, I was eager to meet with you today because there is something important I would like to discuss with you."

Ionescu almost laughed aloud. He knew exactly why she had come. *The Americans wish to sell me corn and soybeans, but they are too late.* The American ambassador would go away empty-handed this time. Too bad. Such an attractive woman.

"Yes?" he said innocently.

"I want to talk to you about sister cities."

Ionescu blinked. "I beg your pardon?"

"Sister cities. You know—like San Francisco and Osaka, Los Angeles and Bombay, Washington and Bangkok . . ."

"I—I don't understand. What does that have to do with—?"

"Mr. President, it occurred to me that you

could get headlines all over the world if you made Bucharest a sister city of some American city. Think of the excitement it would create. It would get almost as much attention as President Ellison's people-to-people plan. It would be an important step toward world peace. Talk about a bridge between our countries! I wouldn't be surprised if it got you a Nobel Peace Prize."

Ionescu sat there, trying to reorient his thinking. He said cautiously, "A sister city with the United States? It is an interesting idea. What would it involve?"

"Mostly wonderful publicity for you. You would be a hero. It would be your idea. You would pay the city a visit. A delegation from Kansas City would pay *you* a visit."

"Kansas City?"

"That's just a suggestion, of course. I don't think you'd want a big city like New York or Chicago—too commercial. And Los Angeles is already spoken for. Kansas City is Middle America. There are farmers there, like your farmers. People with down-to-earth values, like your people. It would be the act of a great statesman, Mr. President. Your name would be on everyone's lips. No one in Europe has thought of doing this."

He sat there silent. "I—I would naturally have to give this a great deal of thought."

"Naturally."

"Kansas City, Kansas, and Bucharest, Romania." He nodded. "We are a much larger city, of course."

"Of course. Bucharest would be the big sister."

"I must admit it is a very intriguing idea."

In fact the more Ionescu thought about it, the more he liked it. *My name will be on everyone's lips. And it will serve to keep the Soviet bear hug from becoming too tight.*

"Is there any chance of a rejection from the American side?" Ionescu asked.

"Absolutely none. I can guarantee it."

He sat there, reflecting. "When would this go into effect?"

"Just as soon as you're ready to announce it. I'll handle our end. You're already a great statesman, Mr. President, but this would make you even greater."

Ionescu thought of something else. "We could set up a trade exchange with our sister city. Romania has many things to sell. Tell me—what crops does Kansas grow?"

"Among other things," Mary said innocently, "corn and soybeans."

* * *

When Stanton Rogers heard the news, he telephoned Mary. "You're a miracle worker," he laughed. "We thought we'd lost that deal. How in the world did you do it?"

"Ego," Mary said. "His."

"The President asked me to tell you what a really great job you're doing over there, Mary."

"Thank him for me, Stan."

The daily long lines in front of the embassy continued to disturb Mary. She discussed it again with Mike Slade.

"There must be something we can do to help those people get out of the country."

"Everything's been tried," Mike assured her. "We've applied pressure, we've offered to sweeten the money pot—the answer is no. Ionescu refuses to cut a deal. The poor bastards are stuck. He has no intention of letting them go. The iron curtain isn't just *around* the country—it's *in* the country."

"I'm going to have a talk with Ionescu again."

"Good luck."

Mary asked Dorothy Stone to set up an appointment with the dictator.

A few minutes later, the secretary walked

into Mary's office. "I'm sorry, Madam Ambassador. No appointments."

Mary looked at her, puzzled. "What does that mean?"

"I'm not sure. Something weird is going on at the palace. Ionescu isn't seeing anybody. In fact, no one can even get into the palace."

Mary sat there, trying to figure out what it could be. Was Ionescu preparing to make a major announcement of some kind? Was a coup imminent? Something important must be happening. Whatever it was, Mary knew she had to find out.

"Dorothy," she said, "you have contacts over at the presidential palace, don't you?"

Dorothy smiled. "You mean the 'old-girl network'? Sure. We talk to one another."

"I'd like you to find out what's going on there . . ."

An hour later, Dorothy reported back. "I found out what you wanted to know," she said. "They're keeping it very hush-hush."

"Keeping what hush-hush?"

"Ionescu's son is dying."

Mary was aghast. "Nicu? What happened?"

"He has botulism poisoning."

Mary asked quickly, "You mean there's an epidemic here in Bucharest?"

"No, ma'am. Do you remember the epidemic they had in East Germany recently? Apparently Nicu visited there and someone gave him some canned food as a gift. He ate some of it yesterday."

"But there's an antiserum for that!" Mary exclaimed.

"The European countries are out of it. The epidemic last month used it all up."

"Oh, my God."

When Dorothy left the office, Mary sat there thinking. It might be too late, but still . . . She remembered how cheerful and happy young Nicu was. He was fourteen years old—only two years older than Beth.

She pressed the intercom button and said, "Dorothy, get me the Centers for Disease Control in Atlanta, Georgia."

Five minutes later she was speaking to the director.

"Yes, Madam Ambassador, we have an antiserum for botulism poisoning, but we haven't had any cases reported in the United States."

"I'm not in the United States," Mary told him. "I'm in Bucharest. I need that serum immediately."

There was a pause. "I'll be happy to supply some," the director said, "but botulism poisoning works very rapidly. I'm afraid that by the time it gets there . . ."

"I'll arrange for it to get here," Mary said, "Just have it ready. Thank you."

Ten minutes later she was speaking to Air Force General Ralph Zukor in Washington.

"Good morning, Madam Ambassador. Well, this is an unexpected pleasure. My wife and I are big fans of yours. How are—?"

"General, I need a favor."

"Certainly. Anything you want."

"I need your fastest jet."

"I beg your pardon?"

"I need a jet to fly some serum to Bucharest right away."

"I see."

"Can you do it?"

"Well, yes. I'll tell you what you have to do. You'll have to get the approval of the secretary of defense. There are some requisition forms for you to fill out. One copy should go to me and another copy to the Department of Defense. We'll send those on to—"

Mary listened, seething. "General—let me tell you what *you* have to do. You have to stop talking and get that damned jet up in the air. If—"

"There's no way that—"

"A boy's life is at stake. And the boy happens to be the son of the president of Romania."

"I'm sorry, but I can't authorize—"

"General, if that boy dies because some form hasn't been filled out, I promise you that I'm going to call the biggest press conference you've ever seen. I'll let you explain why you let Ionescu's son die."

"I can't possibly authorize an operation like this without an approval from the White House. If—"

Mary snapped, "Then get it. The serum will be waiting at the Atlanta airport. And, General—every single minute counts."

She hung up and sat there, silently praying.

General Ralph Zukor's aide said, "What was that all about, sir?"

General Zukor said, "The ambassador expects me to send up an SR-71 to fly some serum to Romania."

The aide smiled. "I'm sure she has no idea of what's involved, General."

"Obviously. But we might as well cover ourselves. Get me Stanton Rogers."

Five minutes later the general was speaking to the president's foreign adviser. "I just wanted to go on record with you that the request was made, and I naturally refused. If—"

Stanton Rogers said, "General, how soon can you have an SR-71 airborne?"

"In ten minutes, but—"

"Do it."

Nicu Ionescu's nervous system had been affected. He lay in bed, disoriented, sweating and pale, attached to a respirator. There were three doctors at his bedside.

President Ionescu strode into his son's bedroom. "What's happening?"

"Your Excellency, we have communicated with our colleagues all over Eastern and Western Europe. There is no antiserum left."

"What about the United States?"

The doctor shrugged. "By the time we could arrange for someone to fly the serum here—" he paused delicately, "I'm afraid it would be too late."

Ionescu walked over to the bed and picked up his son's hand. It was moist and clammy. "You're not going to die," Ionescu wept. "You're not going to die."

When the jet touched down at Atlanta International Airport, an air force limousine was waiting with the antibotulism serum, packed in ice. Three minutes later the jet was back in the air, on a northeast heading.

The SR-71—the air force's fastest supersonic jet—flies at three times the speed of sound. It slowed down once to refuel over the mid-Atlantic. The plane made the five-thousand-mile flight to Bucharest in a little over two and a half hours.

Colonel McKinney was waiting at the airport. An army escort cleared the way to the presidential palace.

Mary had remained in her office all night, getting up-to-the-minute reports on developments. The last report came in at six A.M.

Colonel McKinney telephoned. "They gave the boy the serum. The doctors say he's going to live."

"Oh, thank God!"

Two days later, a diamond-and-emerald necklace was delivered to Mary's office with a note:

I can never thank you enough.
                    Alexandru Ionescu

"My God!" Dorothy exclaimed when she saw the necklace. "It must have cost half a million dollars!"

"At least," Mary said. "Return it."

The following morning, President Ionescu sent for Mary.

An aide said, "The president is waiting for you in his office."

"May I see Nicu first?"

"Yes, of course." He led her upstairs.

Nicu was lying in bed, reading. He looked up as Mary entered. "Good morning, Madam Ambassador."

"Good morning, Nicu."

"My father told me what you did. I wish to thank you."

Mary said, "I couldn't let you die. I'm saving you for Beth one day."

Nicu laughed. "Bring her over and we'll talk about it."

President Ionescu was waiting for Mary downstairs. He said without preamble, "You returned my gift."

"Yes, Your Excellency."

He indicated a chair. "Sit down." He studied her a moment. "What do you want?"

Mary said, "I don't make trades for children's lives."

"You saved my son's life. I must give you something."

"You don't owe me anything, Your Excellency."

Ionescu pounded his fist on the desk. "I will not be indebted to you! Name your price."

Mary said, "Your Excellency, there is no price. I have two children of my own. I know how you must feel."

He closed his eyes for a moment. "Do you? Nicu is my only son. If anything had happened to him—" He stopped, unable to go on.

"I went upstairs to see him. He looks fine." She rose. "If there's nothing else, Your Excellency, I have an appointment back at the embassy." She started to leave.

"Wait!"

Mary turned.

"You will not accept a gift?"

"No. I've explained—"

Ionescu held up a hand. "All right, all right." He thought for a moment. "If you were to make a wish, what would you wish for?"

"There is nothing—"

"You must! I insist! One wish. Anything you want."

Mary stood there, studying his face, thinking. Finally she said, "I wish that the restriction on the Jews waiting to leave Romania could be lifted."

Ionescu sat there, listening to her words. His fingers drummed on the desk. "I see." He was still for a long time. Finally he looked up at Mary. "It shall be done. They will not all be allowed out, of course, but—I will make it easier."

When the announcement was made public two days later, Mary received a telephone call from President Ellison himself.

"By God," he said, "I thought I was sending over a diplomat, and I got a miracle worker."

"I was just lucky, Mr. President."

"It's the kind of luck I wish all my diplomats had. I want to congratulate you, Mary, on everything you've been doing over there."

"Thank you, Mr. President."

She hung up, feeling a warm glow.

Questions for the Reader

Thinking About the Story

1. What was interesting to you about the selections from *Windmills of the Gods*?

2. Were there ways the events or people in the selections became important or special to you? Write about or discuss these.

3. What do you think were the most important things Sidney Sheldon wanted to say in the selections?

4. In what ways did the selections answer the questions you had before you began reading or listening?

5. Were any parts of the selections difficult to understand? If so, you may want to read or listen to them again. Discuss with your learning partners possible reasons why they were difficult.

Thinking About the Writing

1. How did Sidney Sheldon help you see, hear and feel what happened in the selections? Find

the word, phrases or sentences that did this best.

2. Writers think carefully about their stories' settings, characters and events. In writing these selections, which of these things do you think Sidney Sheldon felt was most important? Find the parts of the story that support your opinion.

3. In the selections, Sidney Sheldon uses dialogue. Dialogue can make a story stronger and more alive. Pick out some dialogue that you feel is strong, and explain how it helps the story.

4. The selections from *Windmills of the Gods* are written from the point of view of someone outside the story who tells us what is happening. The writer uses the words "he" and "she" as opposed to "I" or "me." What difference does this create in the writing of the selection?

5. Sidney Sheldon, through his writing, makes us understand some of the fast-moving events in an ambassador's life. Find some parts in the selections that helped you understand how quickly an ambassador must think and act.

Activities

1. Were there any words that were difficult for you in the selections from *Windmills of the*

Gods? Go back to these words and try to figure out their meanings. Discuss what you think each word means, and why you made that guess. Look them up in a dictionary and see if your definitions are the same or different.

Discuss with your learning partners how you are going to remember each word. Some ways to remember words are to put them on file cards, write them in a journal or create a personal dictionary. Be sure to use the words in your writing in a way that will help you to remember their meanings.

2. Talking with other people about what you have read can increase your understanding. Discussion can help you organize your thoughts, get new ideas and rethink your original ideas. Discuss your thoughts about the selections with someone else who has read them. Find out if you helped yourself understand the selections in the same or different ways. Find out if your opinions about the selections are the same or different. See if your thoughts change as a result of this discussion.

3. After you finish reading or listening, you might want to write down your thoughts about the book. You could write your reflections on the book in a journal, or you could write about topics the book has brought up that you want to explore further. You could write a book

review or a letter to a friend who you think might be interested in the book.

4. Did reading the selections give you any ideas for your own writing? You might want to write about:

   • what you would do if you suspected someone of being a spy.
   • facing the challenge of a new job.
   • adjusting to living in a different place.

5. Look in newspapers, magazines and on television for more information about countries in Eastern Europe. You might want to write a piece about current events in these countries or talk about this information with your learning partners.

6. Talk to someone who has lived in another country or someone who came to live in the United States from another country. What did they notice was different? What did they miss from home? How did they adjust?

7. If you could talk to Sidney Sheldon, what questions would you ask about his writing? You might want to write the questions in a journal.

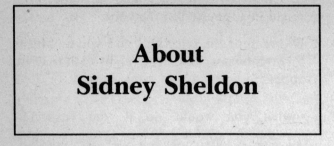

About
Sidney Sheldon

Sidney Sheldon is one of the most widely known authors in the world. Over 100 million copies of his books are in print in 30 countries.

Sheldon was born in Chicago in the 1930s. He says that it was a miracle he became a writer. Both of his parents were third-grade dropouts. "My father never read a book in his life," he recalls, "and I was the only one in my family to complete high school."

Sheldon went to Hollywood when he was 17 years old. Sheldon got a job reading scripts at Universal Studios. He eventually became a screenwriter at Republic studios where they made low-budget movies.

When World War II broke out, Sheldon became a pilot in the air force. After he was discharged, he came to New York City to write plays. He was a top playwright by the time he was 25.

He went on to become a successful screenwriter at MGM Studios. He wrote more than 30 films, including *Easter Parade* (1948), which starred Judy Garland and Fred Astaire. He won an Academy Award for *The Bachelor and the Bobby Soxer* (1947), starring Cary Grant.

He became involved with television when it was a new industry. He created *The Patty Duke Show*, *I Dream of Jeannie* and *Hart to Hart*.

His first novel, *The Naked Face,* was turned down by five publishers before it was finally accepted and published in 1976. The book was a critical success and won an Edgar Allan Poe Award.

The author researches each of his books in great detail. Very often Sheldon will spend a year traveling in several foreign countries, exploring interesting customs and places. Sheldon says, "If you read about one of my characters eating a meal in a restaurant in some exotic part of the world, you can bet I've had that very meal in that same restaurant."

Sheldon works six days a week on his writing. It takes him 12 to 18 months to write, edit and rewrite a manuscript before he finally sends it to his publisher. "I feel obligated to make these books as good as I know how," he says.

Sidney Sheldon lives in southern California.

MAP OF COMMUNIST COUNTRIES
AND WESTERN ALLIES IN EUROPE IN 1987

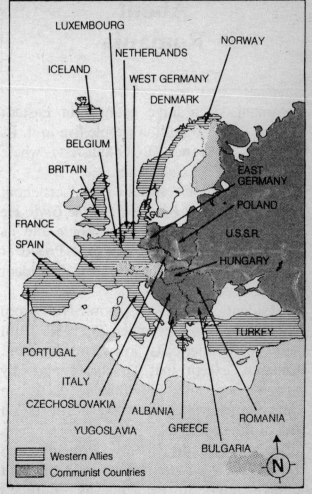

About Romania

Romania is a large country in Eastern Europe. Over 20 million people live in it. Its capital is Bucharest (BOO-kuh-rest), where *Windmills of the Gods* is set.

Sidney Sheldon researched the facts about Romania to write *Windmills of the Gods.* He read about its president, its people and its places. He modeled the fictional President Alexandru Ionescu on the real President Nicolae Ceausescu.

President Ceausescu (chow-SHESS-koo) was executed on December 25, 1989. Until then, few Americans knew much about Romania, except that Dracula supposedly carried out his bloodthirsty deeds in Transylvania, which is in the northwestern part of the country.

For most of its history, Romania was controlled by other countries. President Ionescu refers to Romania as "Europe's doormat" on page 26 of the story. It was only in 1920 that the independent Romanian state as we know it today was formed.

In 1948, Romania allied with the Soviet Union and pledged to follow its path to become a Communist society. In doing this, Romania joined the other Eastern European countries that were pledged to Communism. These Communist countries were allied against the democratic countries of Western Europe and the United States.

A Communist society is based on the belief that the government should own the farms, factories and other means of production and that the goods be equally distributed to all the citizens. A Communist government is run by one political party.

Ceausescu worked his way up through the ranks of the Communist Party in the late 1940s and 1950s. Ceausescu became Romania's leader in 1965.

He didn't join the Soviet Union in many aspects of the cold war against the democratic countries. Romania, an oil-producing nation, began to sell gasoline to the democratic countries. One result of this policy was that the Western nations began to do business with Romania. In 1969, American President Richard Nixon made an official trip to

Romania and President Ceausescu came to the United States.

At home Ceausescu appointed over 30 members of his family, including his wife, to key government posts. In the 1960s, statues and pictures of Ceausescu appeared throughout the country. Bookstores were forced to display the books he wrote and collections of the speeches he made. Hours of television time were devoted to him.

Most important, no one could write or say anything that was in any way critical of him, his family or the government. He even required that all typewriters be registered with the police. In this way, they could track down anyone who wrote against the government.

He was able to control the country because he ran the army, and, more important, the Securitate, the secret police. Founded in 1945, it eventually grew to become a force of 180,000.

The Securitate served several functions: It guarded the members of the Communist Party's Central Committee, patrolled the country's borders, guarded political prisoners and protected the Ceausescu family.

In the 1970s, Ceausescu started an

expensive building program. Beautiful and historic buildings, especially in Bucharest, were bulldozed. In their place, huge concrete buildings were erected.

By 1983, the government owed an enormous amount of money to foreign countries that had made loans to finance the new buildings. In order to pay back the loans, Romania had to sell food and fuel to other countries. This caused severe shortages at home. Food was scarce and rationed. Cities were dark at night and buildings went unheated.

Although Ceausescu had paid back half the debt by 1988, the Romanian people did not want to continue under such harsh conditions. When people tried to express their dissatisfaction, the demonstrators were crushed by the army and the Securitate. On December 16, 1989, while President Ceausescu was out of the country, a huge crowd gathered in the city of Timişoara (tee-mee-SHWA-ruh) in western Romania. The crowds shouted "Freedom!" and "Down with the dictator!" The armed forces moved in, but this time the people convinced some of the soldiers to join them in their fight for freedom. It is believed that thousands of civilians were killed and wounded in these demonstrations.

Five days later, Ceausescu was back in the country and the demonstrations spread to Bucharest, the capital. Realizing that the situation was hopeless, Ceausescu and his wife tried to escape from the city. They were caught, tried and then executed on December 25, 1989.

Today the Romanian people, like those in other countries in Eastern Europe, are working to establish new and free forms of government. They have broken away from the Soviet Union. A new era has begun in Eastern Europe.

About Bestsellers

Windmills of the Gods was first published in hardcover in 1987. Over 700,000 copies of this edition were sold. It came out in paperback less than a year later. More than 4,500,000 copies of the paperback edition have been sold. And the book will continue to sell in large numbers far into the future.

Books that sell in these huge numbers are called bestsellers. Sidney Sheldon is one of a small number of authors whose books become bestsellers.

Most books that are published do not become bestsellers. There are about 50,000 new books published each year in the United States. Of these, only about 64 titles are on a bestseller list at any one time.

Many newspapers print bestseller lists based on reports from bookstores in their areas. But the bestseller list most people refer to when they talk about bestsellers is the one published by *The New York Times*. The *Times* prints two lists, one for new paperbacks and one for new hardcovers, in its Sunday book review section. These lists are read by librarians, booksellers and book buyers who use them to help decide what books to buy and sell.

Each list has two parts. The first part shows the top 15 fiction books. This is the part of the list where Sidney Sheldon's books appear. The second part of the list is for nonfiction titles. These are biography, travel, business, sports, advice, history, science, cooking and other factual titles.

To find out each week which books have sold the most copies, The *Times* gets sales figures from booksellers all over the country.

Why does a book become a bestseller? What makes millions of people buy a copy of one book?

One reason may be that the author is a celebrity. Bill Cosby, Jane Fonda and Shirley Maclaine are well-known entertainers whose books have been on bestseller lists. Many book buyers enjoy reading about what celebrities think and feel about themselves and their lives. In their imaginations, these readers can share the lives of the famous by buying and reading their books.

Biographies, books written about famous people such as Martin Luther King, Jr. or

Elvis Presley, also sell well for the same reasons.

Good publicity can often get millions of people to buy a book. When an author is interviewed on a popular television show like *Oprah* or *Phil Donahue*, the television audience may get very excited about or interested in the author's book. And when the "Dear Abby" column recommends a book, millions of her readers may want to get that title.

For fiction titles such as those that Sidney Sheldon writes, some become bestsellers because the author has developed a "following." Sidney Sheldon has written many books, and his readers eagerly wait for his newest book to be published. As soon as it is published, these readers go to bookstores and libraries to get the book. Some other authors who have huge followings are Stephen King, Mary Higgins Clark and Danielle Steel.

A fiction title may become a bestseller or sell even more copies when a movie or television special is based on it. All of Sidney Sheldon's books have been made into movies or television specials. Whenever one appears, people who did not know about his books are motivated to go out and read the story that the movie was based on.

Nonfiction books outsell fiction books by two to one. Some of the most popular nonfiction books are reference books and books about child care, cooking and religion. *Dr. Spock's Baby & Child Care* has sold over 30 million copies. *The Better Homes and Gardens Cook Book* has sold over 21 million copies. Not surprisingly, the biggest bestseller of all time is the Bible. But because it is published in so many editions, no one knows exactly how many millions of copies have been sold.

Publishers Weekly
HARDCOVER BESTSELLERS
JANUARY 20, 1989

FICTION	Last Week	Weeks on List
1 **The Sands of Time.** Sidney Sheldon. Morrow, $19.95.	1	8
2 **The Cardinal of the Kremlin.** Tom Clancy. Putnam, $19.95.	2	23
3 **Alaska.** James Michener. Random House, $22.50.	3	28
4 **One.** Richard Bach. Morrow/Silver Arrow Books, $16.95.	4	11
5 **The Queen of the Damned.** Anne Rice. Knopf, $18.95.	5	12
6 **Breathing Lessons.** Anne Tyler. Knopf, $18.95.	7	16
7 **Spy Hook.** Len Deighton. Knopf, $18.95.	8	3

A bestseller list from <u>Publishers Weekly</u> magazine.

WRITERS' VOICES

Kareem Abdul-Jabbar and Peter Knobler, *Selected from GIANT STEPS*

Rudolfo A. Anaya, *Selected from BLESS ME, ULTIMA*

Maya Angelou, *Selected from I KNOW WHY THE CAGED BIRD SINGS and THE HEART OF A WOMAN*

Peter Benchley, *Selected from JAWS*

Ray Bradbury, *Selected from DARK THEY WERE, AND GOLDEN-EYED*

Carol Burnett, *Selected from ONE MORE TIME*

Mary Higgins Clark, *Selected from THE LOST ANGEL*

Avery Corman, *Selected from KRAMER vs. KRAMER*

Bill Cosby, *Selected from FATHERHOOD and TIME FLIES*

Louise Erdrich, *Selected from LOVE MEDICINE*

Alex Haley, *Selected from A DIFFERENT KIND OF CHRISTMAS*

Maxine Hong Kingston, *Selected from CHINA MEN and THE WOMAN WARRIOR*

Loretta Lynn with George Vecsey, *Selected from COAL MINER'S DAUGHTER*

Mark Mathabane, *Selected from KAFFIR BOY*

Gloria Naylor, *Selected from THE WOMEN OF BREWSTER PLACE*

Priscilla Beaulieu Presley with Sandra Harmon, *Selected from ELVIS AND ME*

Mario Puzo, *Selected from THE GODFATHER*

Ahmad Rashad with Peter Bodo, *Selected from RASHAD*

Sidney Sheldon, *Selected from WINDMILLS OF THE GODS*

Anne Tyler, *Selected from THE ACCIDENTAL TOURIST*

Abigail Van Buren, *Selected from THE BEST OF DEAR ABBY*

Tom Wolfe, *Selected from THE RIGHT STUFF*

SELECTED FROM CONTEMPORARY AMERICAN PLAYS

SELECTED FROM 20th-CENTURY AMERICAN POETRY

Books are $3.50 each. To order, please send your check to Publishing Program, Literacy Volunteers of New York City, 121 Avenue of the Americas, New York, NY 10013. Please add $2.00 per order and .50 per book to cover postage and handling. NY and NJ residents, add appropriate sales tax. Prices subject to change without notice.